Text Copyright © 2023 Jean Ward

Illustration Copyright © 2023 Phillip Reed

All rights reserved. No part of this book may be reproduced or used in

any manner without written permission of the copyright owner
except for the use of quotations in a book review.

For more information email info@phillipreed.net

DO YOU KNOW WHERE I LIVE?

A BOOK ABOUT ANIMAL HOMES

Written by Jean Ward

Illustrated by Phillip Reed

Contents

Chapter 1: Homes ... 1

Chapter 2: The Hedgehog ... 2

Chapter 3: The Grey Squirrel ... 4

Chapter 4: The Brown Hare ... 6

Chapter 5: The Rabbit ... 8

Chapter 6: The Fox ... 10

Chapter 7: The Otter ... 12

Chapter 8: The Red Deer ... 14

Chapter 9: The Badger ... 16

Chapter 10: The Prairie Dog and The Chimpanzee ... 18

Chapter 11: Lack of Homes and Loss of Habitat ... 22

Chapter 12: Ideas You Might Like to Try ... 24

Glossary ... 25

References and Acknowledgements ... 26

Chapter 1: Homes

This book is about homes. You have a home, and I have one. But what *is* a home and why do we need one? A home is a special place that humans and almost all mammals have, where they feel safe, are protected, looked after and loved – where they are taught, usually by parents, how to become independent adults. Throughout the world, depending on climate, landscape and available building materials, and what they are needed for, homes can be very different and they all have their own names. Here in England, we have houses, flats, castles, palaces, cottages, hostels and bungalows. In some countries, people may live in tents or caves and in the Arctic, where it is below freezing for much of the year, huge slabs of frozen snow can be used to make homes called igloos.

Most animals make or find a place for their home. Some may return to the same home year after year, whilst others make a new one each day, then leave it and move on. These animal homes often have special names, many of them coming from very old books written six to seven hundred years ago. Sometimes, if the writers, and later the printers, made a mistake, over years, the words became slightly changed, so the names we use today may be different, but similar to the original old ones. Often the home-name describes the shape, situation or position of the home.

Chapter 2: The Hedgehog

Weight: Up to 2kgs – heaviest before hibernation

Height: 6 – 8cms up to shoulder

Home: HIBERNACULUM

Hedgehogs are found all over the UK except in Northern Scotland and on high ground. They have short legs, a short tail and a sharp pointed face. The head and body are covered by brownish grey spikes, which stand upright when the hedgehog rolls into a ball, if startled or attacked.

During the day in summer, the hedgehog hides away in tall grass, under leaves or bushes. They are nocturnal and at night become very active scurrying about as they hunt for insects, the eggs of ground nesting birds, snails and worms.

It is in winter that hedgehogs make a safe nest-like place where they can sleep during the cold months. This home, or hibernaculum, is made of dry leaves and grass and can be under log piles and old boxes. If there is a warm period, the hedgehog may wake up, have a wander, a nibble, and may even make another cosy hibernaculum for the rest of the winter.

Nowadays, hedgehogs are attracted to the wooden hedgehog boxes where they stay safe and dry during their hibernation.

HIBERNACULUM comes from a Latin word 'hibernus' which means 'winter', so it is a winter home for both hedgehogs and amphibians.

Chapter 3: The Grey Squirrel

Length: 23 – 30 cms to rump (19 – 25 cms tail length)
Height: 20 – 30 cms when sitting upright

Home: DREY

The grey squirrel was brought from America to England over one hundred and fifty years ago and is now found all over the UK. They are dark grey with a long bushy tail, and although they fight and kill the smaller red squirrels, they can become quite tame in gardens and parks.

The squirrel's home, or drey, is a round bundle of vegetation about the size of a football. It is made of twigs mixed with strips of bark and clumps of mosses and leaves. The entrance is on the side of the ball and this may be filled in if it is very cold, and also if the mother has to leave the young ones whilst she goes out to find food. The drey is made in the branches of trees, and sometimes in the hollows of old trees. Although squirrels hide nuts and fruit, they seldom go back to eat them. They tend to forget where they have hidden them. However, they are experts at finding their way into bird feeders!! The young, born naked and blind, are fed by the mother and can breed when one year old. The first winter they all sleep together in the drey, the mother having left once they became independent.

Large nest boxes can be placed between the branches and young squirrels are born here, well-protected.

DREY / DRAY – little is known about the old meaning of this word.

Chapter 4: The Brown Hare

Length: 48 – 75 cms to rump

Weight: 2.5 – 7kgs

Home: FORM

The brown hare is like a large rabbit, with long ears and a white tail, both tipped with black. They are found on low-lying farmland all over the UK. Hares have long back legs, can run very fast and are good protective mothers. Females (does) will stand on their back legs and 'box' to frighten away other female intruders.

Hares do not make a nest but search for a sheltered place in the sun where they can see around them. They make a flattened area to the shape of their body which gradually becomes deeper and more curved. Sometimes they scrape and hollow out an area where they sleep and rest. This area is called a form. The young hares (leverets) are born together, but later the mother, carrying them in her mouth, takes each to its own separate form, where they lie alone and still, as if they have been abandoned. But the mother knows where they are and at dusk gathers them together for their daily meal. This continues for about one month, by which time they are independent.

FORM – From a Latin word, forma, meaning a shape or mould, curved like a shallow bowl.

Chapter 5: The Rabbit

Length: 40 cms

Height: 14 – 18 cms

Home: BURROW / WARREN

A rabbit is very similar to a hare, but is smaller and has shorter ears with no black tips. Unlike hares, they are very common and are found throughout Britain wherever there is grass.

Rabbits, who are very good at digging, live in large, long underground tunnels called warrens. These have entrances 10 - 20cms in diameter, and can easily be spotted by the well cropped grass and droppings nearby.

Before she has her babies, the female rabbit (doe) usually leaves the warren and digs a burrow or breeding spot. This slopes downwards for about a metre and then levels out to become up to a metre or so long. She is a good mother and to keep the babies warm and safe, she lines the burrow with her own fur. When she is away, so as to hide the entrance, she blocks it with grass and leaves. From being totally dependent at birth, young rabbits are fully independent within one month.

In warm weather, rabbits will find a sheltered area and flatten it to make a resting place, or form, but normally they stay underground during the day and come out at night and early morning to feed and play.

BURROW – a hole dug in the ground for shelter and safety. It comes from an old English word, beorgan, which means to protect. Several burrows can link together to make a warren which can extend over a large area.

Chapter 6: The Fox

Length: 45 – 90 cms to rump (32 – 53 cms tail length)
Height: 35 – 50 cms to shoulder

Home: EARTH

The fox is similar to a medium sized dog, with a reddish brown back, grey belly and a long, wide, bushy, darker brown tail with a white tip. They are common all over the UK, and nowadays are often seen in towns where they feed from rubbish bins and thrown out scraps. These town foxes are called feral foxes and they hide under sheds and behind garden shrubs. They make their earths in rubbish tips, junk yards, or under woodwork.

In fine weather, 'wild' foxes rest above ground, sheltered by bushes and tall grass. If they are undisturbed, they may flatten this area so it becomes a shallow bowl, the shape of their body. In bad weather, foxes hide under roots and rocks.

It is when the female fox, (vixen), is about to have cubs that she looks for a suitable place to give birth. She does not usually dig her own earth, except in very loose, sandy soil, but adapts the holes of badgers and rabbits, blocking up and hiding all but one entrance. In this quiet peaceful place the mother fox feeds her small blind cubs for about one month, then they begin to come out and are fed rats and mice. As they grow, the area around the earth becomes flattened, worn and messy, and there may be signs of black fox poo (scat) and remains of old food. Once the cubs become more mobile, they often all leave that earth and find a new one or maybe just a sheltered place where there is more available food.

The cubs are not fully independent until they are twelve to eighteen months old, although by six months they are hunting for their own food.

EARTH – an old English word which was used six to seven hundred years ago. First it was spelt eorthe, then it became nerthe and finally earth. Earth means a hiding place under the ground. It is also the name given to our planet, the third in order of distance from the Sun.

Chapter 7: The Otter

Length: 65 – 75 cms to rump (40 – 50 cms tail length)
Height: 14 – 20 cms

Home: HOLT

Otters are shy creatures, seldom seen but detected by their web-footed tracks. They have strong short legs and a large tail, used when swimming. Often called the engineers of the river, otters are very skilled at moving logs and branches to make dams. They come out at night, usually in couples, and are very strong, agile hunters. They eat fish, eels, snakes, ducks and have been known to tackle and kill a sheep.

Otters rest above the ground in holes, and under rocks and logs. These resting places are called lie-ups, or couches, but it is the holt that is the otter's real home. These are usually in stream banks, under roots with an underwater entrance and often an exit above ground. There are usually two chambers, one used as a toilet and the other where they sleep, curled up like a dog. There may be an otter run leading to the holt, with remains of food, e.g. fish fins and rabbit bones. The young born in the holt, are blind, with a soft coat. They are fully independent at six months.

To increase the number of otters, they are being bred in protected areas and then released into their safe natural habitat.

HOLT is a very old word meaning a small wood, a place of shelter. It was in America that 'holt' began to be used to mean the home of an otter.

Chapter 8: The Red Deer

Length: 1.8 – 2 metres to rump

Height: 0.95 – 1.3 metres at shoulder

Home: LIE

Many types of deer live in the UK, but the red deer is considered the true wild deer. It is common in Northern Scotland and can sometimes be seen in England in wooded areas. Red deer are larger than the other park deer, which have been brought here from other countries. A red deer herd may have its own territory, but generally males and females tend to live separately within that area.

Red deer do not construct a proper home, but rest in the same patch of woodland, usually on the edge of a field. The chosen area is called a lie, and they may return to it day after day, and then make a fresh one when the herd moves on. A lie can be recognised as an area of flattened vegetation, such as tall grass and bracken. The surrounding ground may have been scraped bare and bean-shaped droppings are often scattered around.

The red deer is very cautious and relies on its sense of smell to warn of danger. With help from the wind, they can smell a human over one mile away, and if they sense anything strange, will soon be off into the undergrowth. The calves are born in a well-hidden lie and for the first week are unable to stand, so the mother (hind) visits to feed them. They start to follow her at two months, remaining with her until they are two years old.

LIE – a place where animals choose to rest, lie down, or just look around, making sure they are safe. It comes from an old English word, liegan, which was in use seven hundred years ago.

Chapter 9: The Badger

Length: 75 cms 5 cms tail length

Height: 30 cms at shoulder

Home: SETT

The badger is found throughout most of the UK. It is bear-like, with big wide shoulders and a curved back, covered by longish black/grey hair. Its white face has a black streak down each side. Badgers are very strong nocturnal animals, and they dig out a sett in soft soil, at the edge of a wood or at the bottom of an old hedge. They stay in the sett until it is dark, but in very cold winters, may partially hibernate. The path leading to an old much-used sett is well marked with little vegetation and sometimes has a marmite-y smell. The sett can have entrances of over 30 cm in diameter, and there can be 30 to 40 entrances at different levels along the bank. Piles of dug-out soil (spoils) indicate badgers are active. Some entrances widen out into large chambers where several families live together. Foxes and rabbits may also share the home.

Before the cubs are born, there is a spring clean and all the bedding is dragged out and the chamber relined with fresh ferns and grass. The badger takes the clean bedding between its forefeet and holds it in place with its chin, and shuffles backwards down the entrance. Far from the sett, the badger digs an "earth closet" so there is no dung in or near the sett. Before the mother enters, she cleans her claws on a tree – cleaner than we are! When they are born, the cubs are blind, silver-grey and helpless, and don't come out until two months old. Their mother is very caring and gentle, keeping the cubs well fed and clean.

When it is almost dark, the parents emerge, looking around, making sure it is safe for the cubs to come out. During night-walks (of up to 10 km), they play, scratch and hunt, eating fruit, honey, roots, slugs, snails, insects, snakes and young birds. In the UK, badger setts are protected by law, and should never be disturbed.

SETT: It may come from an old Norwegian word, "setja", an old English word, "setten", or a French word, "settle". All mean a seat.

Chapter 10: The Prairie Dog and The Chimpanzee

Neither of these mammals are found in the UK, but are included as they both have interesting ways of living and home building.

The Prairie Dog

Length: About 25 cms plus tail

Weight: Up to 1 kg

Height: 35 – 40 cms when standing upright

Home: TOWN

Prairie dogs have a face similar to a guinea pig, but with a long body and short legs. They live in the open grasslands of North America, hundreds of them together in a huge network of underground tunnels that can stretch for kilometres. The many entrances, or burrows, lead into a maze of tunnels, which are divided into areas for sleeping, toileting and nurseries for the young ones. This whole system is known as a town, busy and bustling underground. On the surface, they build tall, pointed mounds which look like chimneys, allowing fresh air to enter the town. Prairie dogs live as a group, and several stay above ground on watch duty, looking out for dangers. If necessary, they warn the others, who dive into the nearest hole for safety.

TOWN – the word comes from an old Norwegian word ton, that means an enclosure. Some of our towns have this ending: Brigh<u>ton</u>, Middle<u>ton</u>, New<u>ton</u> (New Town).

Chapter 10: The Prairie Dog and The Chimpanzee (continued)

The Chimpanzee

Weight: Males 40 – 70 kgs

Height: 170 cms

Home: SLEEPING PLATFORM

Chimpanzees live high up in the dense forests of West Africa. At night, to keep safe and warm, they make a nest or sleeping platform up in the tree tops. They fold bendy branches over and over to form a flat area, strong enough to sleep on. To soften it, they cover the platform with leaves and may sleep on it for several nights, or may make a new one in another area. The mother chimp teaches her young how to recognise the ironwood tree, as this has the best bendy branches for weaving the sleeping platform.

SLEEPING PLATFORM – the word platform comes from a French word plate-forme, meaning flat place.

Chapter 11: Lack of Homes and Loss of Habitat

This chapter explains why sometimes both human beings and animals have difficulty in finding a place to make and call a home.

Almost all people would like a home, but there are many who do not have one. Without a home it is difficult to keep warm and clean, to make food, get a job and to feel safe, with people you trust. People become homeless for various reasons. Their home may have been burnt down, destroyed by an earthquake, or by a bomb. It may have been flooded, or knocked down to make space for a new motorway. Perhaps, if there is a war in their country, to stay safe, they have had to move and leave everything behind. Sometimes there may be a problem in their home and they don't want to live there anymore, but cannot find anywhere else. Whatever the reason, we hope that these homeless people can get help to find new homes, where they can live safe and happy lives.

Animals too are having difficulty finding the right sort of place and materials needed to build their homes. The areas where they live are called their habitats. All over the world, their habitats are being destroyed, mainly by human beings who cut down trees, grow new unsuitable crops, fill in lakes, let ponds dry up and cut down hedges. Without the habitat they need, animals, birds and insects will all die through lack of food, shelter and protection, especially their young.

In Africa, large areas of forest and jungle are being cut down in order to grow crops to sell. This means birds, monkeys, chimps, snakes and all the insects that live in these steamy jungles are having less room to make their homes, and gradually these living creatures will become scarce. In countries where the tall grasslands and shrubs are being cleared and burnt, maybe to build factories or mines, lions, tigers, elephants, leopards and zebras have less habitat in which to hunt their prey, and fewer safe places to raise their young. Once this natural balance is upset, it is difficult to correct.

Here in the UK, in the last fifty years many hedges around small fields were dug up to make one big field. This was better for the large new combine harvester, but certainly not for the birds, the small mammals like mice and voles, or for the hundreds of insects that live in the hedges.

Countries all over the world need to try to change things so that both humans and animals can live safely together in their chosen habitats with food and shelter. Otherwise, these magnificent beasts may gradually disappear, and how sad that would be for your children and grandchildren. However, there are things we can all do to try to prevent this happening. Why not have a go?

Chapter 12: Ideas You Might Like to Try

1.   If you only have a balcony or tiny garden, you may find a place to hang a bird feeder, especially during cold, frosty spells and at nesting times. The parents will feed at the feeder, but if the babies are still in the nest, they will probably be being fed caterpillars rather than food from the feeder. They do get very hungry and the parents get very tired continually flying backwards and forwards with food.

2.   Make holes in the bottom of plastic pots or an old washing-up bowl. Fill them with soil and plant a few seeds. Even the soil will be a home for some tiny insects and flowers could produce pollen for the bees.

3.   If you are lucky enough to have a bigger garden, maybe you could make a little pond, again a bucket or washing-up bowl would be alright. This would provide water for birds, frogs and other creatures like water snails and water boatmen. Have one or two large stones in the water so that frogs can easily get in and out.

4.   Plant a tree that has berries to provide food for birds.

5.   Don't cut grass too often or too short as this helps to prevent it being dried out. Lots of creatures live in the grass and soil and need it damp.

6.   If possible, put up a nest box for garden birds.

7.   Don't use pesticides which kill insects and small animals.

8.   Make a bug hotel. See the National Trust website for instructions.

9.   Make a hibernaculum for a hedgehog using grass, twigs and old wood piled up in a sheltered area.

10.   Make a bee bowl by putting some stones in a shallow dish and pour in some fresh water, leaving the top of the stones above the surface of the water. Bees will be able to land there and have a drink.

Organisations that can give you more help with how to make your own little area a home for insects and animals are:

The RSPB (www.rspb.org.uk)

The Wildlife Trusts (www.wildlifetrusts.org)

The National Trust https://www.nationaltrust.org.uk/features/50-things-to-do-before-youre-11--activity-list

Buglife (www.buglife.org.uk)

GLOSSARY

Agile: Ability to move quickly and easily.

Amphibian: Animals able to live in water and on the land, e.g. toads, newts and frogs

Breed: To produce babies.

Dependent: To rely on a person or thing for help.

Earth Closet: A hole in the ground, sometimes with a shelter around it where humans and animals can poo and then cover it with earth so it doesn't smell.

E.g.: Short way of writing 'for example' (Latin)

Habitat: The normal chosen place where a person, animal or plant is usually found.

Hibernation: To hide away and sleep during the winter.

Independent: To be able to manage alone, without help.

Mammal: An animal that produces milk to feed its young.

Natural: Something that occurs without the influence of man.

Nocturnal: An animal that hunts and becomes active at night.

Original: The first of its kind that has not been copied exactly from something else.

Pesticides: A mixture of chemicals used to kill plants and which often harms and may kill insects and animals too.

Territory: An area that an animal or bird treats as its own.

Vegetation: A mixture of plants, grasses and shrubs all growing together.

Water boatman: A small water insect with long back legs that it uses like oars. It has a boat-shaped body and swims upside down.

Web-footed: The skin between the toes of certain animals and water birds, e.g. ducks, puffins, otters and frogs.

REFERENCES

Nature Watch: How to Track and Observe Wildlife, Simon King (Quadrille Publishing Ltd 2016)

A Beast Book For The Pocket, Edmund Sandars (Oxford University Press 1944)

AKNOWLEDGEMENTS

I would like to thank, Sharon Barker for her valuable help in putting this book together. My two young friends, Deepak Yuvaraj and Elliot Simmonds-Munday for reading the manuscript and for their helpful feedback and all those who showed interest and encouragement me to finish the book. Also, a special thank you to Phillip Reed for his beautiful illustrations and assistance in formatting and self-publishing this book.

Printed in Great Britain
by Amazon